The Arran skyline from Ardrossan

'**D**oon the watter' epitomises the traditional lure for the Glaswegian of the Firth of Clyde and the dramatic islands that once formed 'Buteshire'. Goat Fell, not quite a Munro but worth every one of its 2,866 feet, is chief of the granite hills that give north Arran its 'Sleeping Warrior' outline from the Ayrshire coast. Bute, though less hilly, has its own craggy knolls and sweeping sandy bays. The Cumbraes, Holy Island and distant Ailsa Craig, too, all have their own distinctive and well-loved shapes. This booklet explains how they were fashioned by over 600 million years of geological time.

Granite tor

Although not the oldest rocks in this area, at a mere 60 million years old, the granite hills in the north of Arran are by far the most prominent. At that time Greenland and North America were joined to the north-west coast of Britain, and the Atlantic Ocean was just beginning to open as the Eurasian and North American continents drifted apart. Cracks related to this opening formed down the Firth of Clyde, beginning to detemine the outline of Arran and the sea lochs to the north. It is worth noting that Arran has been an island longer than Britain, which was still joined to the rest of Europe after the last Ice Age.

The continental crust was stretched and thinned along the west coast of Scotland. Molten rock, or magma, exploited points of weakness at centres from Skye to Antrim, forcing columns of magma towards the surface. A dark rock called gabbro was formed at great depth, while higher up the magma cooled to form granite. In many cases the magma reached the surface and built up a massive caldera volcano of lava flows or ash falls, some of which slumped back into the crater. At least three such volcanoes are present in the Clyde region: in north Arran, in central Arran and at Ailsa Craig. Earth movements have raised each of these volcanic centres, but by varying amounts, so the erosive forces of ice, water and wind have worn them down to expose different levels of their volcanic 'roots'.

North Arran

Thin section of granite viewed through a microscope

Erosion in the north of Arran has removed the characteristic volcano shape and worn the rocks down to the level where the molten rock cooled as granite. The granite now stands up as higher ground because it is harder and more resistant to erosion than the surrounding ancient sedimentary rocks, which were tilted when the granite was forced into place.
The northern hills of Arran are in fact made up of two intrusions of granite, an earlier coarser granite which forms the higher hills and a later finer granite in the centre forming the lower ground.

Granite is a crystalline rock. As the molten magma cooled very slowly, crystals formed, and the slower it cooled the more time the crystals had to grow. Most crystals are big enough to see with the naked eye, and give the rock its rough granular surface (good grip for mountaineers). Under a polaroid microscope the different minerals can be recognised: quartz, feldspar and mica.

Like all igneous rocks granite has joints, which are cracks formed when the rock cooled and shrank. In granite the joints weather to give the typical wall-like effect called a tor; this, and the pale grey colour of the granite, makes tors distinctive features of the landscape.

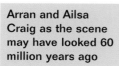

Arran and Ailsa Craig as the scene may have looked 60 million years ago

Other volcanoes

Ailsa Craig

Ailsa Craig is another volcanic centre. Known as Paddy's Milestone because of its position midway between Glasgow and Ireland, Ailsa Craig, sticking above the sea, is all that is presently visible of this ancient volcano. The granite is distinctive and easily recognisable; it contains a blue mineral, riebeckite. Despite its remote location the quality of the rock was so outstanding, particularly for making curling stones, that the island's shape has been altered by quarrying.

The hills of central Arran, lower and less dramatic than those in the north, mark the site of another volcano. This area never rose so high as the northern volcano, so it has been eroded down only to the lower part of the actual volcano, exposing the caldera into which the surface rocks subsided. Hence, there are blocks of lavas and volcanic ash which formed during the volcanic episode, as well as blocks from the overlying Cretaceous chalk and Jurassic marine clays with fossils. It is because the rocks are variable and fragmented that the hills are not so prominent.

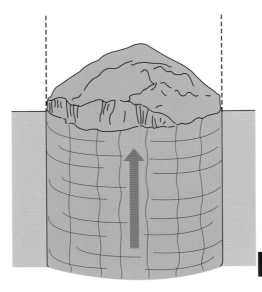

Cross section of granite plug

Sills make cliffs

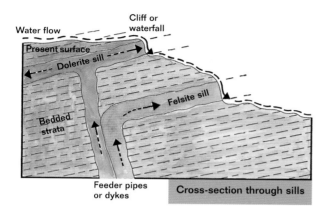

Cross-section through sills

(labels: Water flow; Cliff or waterfall; Present surface; Dolerite sill; Bedded strata; Felsite sill; Feeder pipes or dykes)

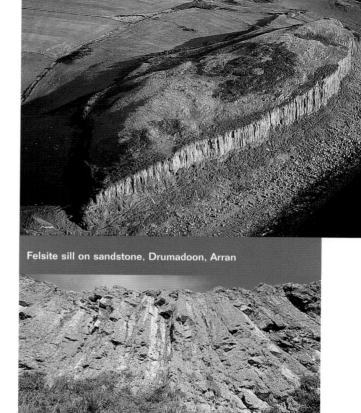

Felsite sill on sandstone, Drumadoon, Arran

Much of the molten rock in a volcano is never in fact erupted as lava flows. Instead of reaching the surface vertically through pipes and cracks, the magma finds an easier route sideways between layers of rock. Eventually it cools as a sandwich of hard crystalline igneous rock, called a sill, between softer layers such as sandstone and mudstone. Many such sills were formed in the red sandstones in the south part of Arran. Some consist of a dark rock called dolerite; others of a light coloured rock, felsite.

As the rocks of Arran have been tilted by earth movements, so the sills are normally inclined rather than horizontal. The effect of erosion on any landscape formed from alternating hard and soft rocks is that the harder layers resist and stand out. Hence most of the hills in the south part of Arran are formed of the harder sill rocks, with the softer rocks in between forming hollows. This leads to a stepped landscape called 'trap featuring', from 'trap', the old word for lava.

Round the coast of Arran the sills form many of the fine cliffs, such as Holy Island, Pladda and Drumadoon. Indeed, the very shape of Arran has been dictated by sills, which form most of the headlands, such as King's Cross Point and Brown Head. Inland, rivers flowing across the stepped landscape produce waterfalls where the sills form resistant layers. Falls such as Glen Ashdale and Auchenhew are a feature of the south Arran landscape.

Dykes, when the islands were stretched and stretched

Another effect of the opening of the Atlantic Ocean was that the land, including the Clyde Islands, was stretched from east to west. The result was cracks running north-south; and molten rock flowed up from the depth into these cracks. They may indeed have erupted as fissure volcanoes such as those which occur in Iceland at present. The crust stretched by as much as 7 per cent. The magma in the cracks solidified underground in vertical sheets, or dykes, of black dolerite. These have been worn down by erosion and are particularly well seen where the black dykes cut red sandstones along the south coast of Arran.

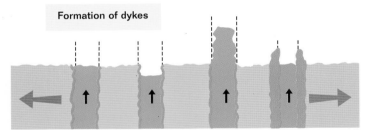

Formation of dykes

Above - Igneous dykes, Arran south coast
Below - Dolerite dykes, Kildonan shore, Arran

The width of the dykes varies from a few centimetres to as much as 30 metres. The dolerite is well jointed and can show spheroidal or onion-skin weathering. On the beach rock platform, the dykes commonly stand a little above the sandstone because they are harder. Sometimes, though, wave action has plucked out the dyke rock. The heat of the magma baked the rock on either side, making it harder than the dyke rock so that in some cases the baked sandstone stands proud.

In earlier times the sea acted in just the same way. Thus dykes were eroded into stacks on what are now the raised beaches. On the Great Cumbrae some of the large dykes form very spectacular wall-like features, such as the Lion Rock and the Diel's Dyke.

Little Cumbrae

Lava 3
Lava 2
Lava 1

Rubbly top with bubbles
Massive jointed centre
Chilled base

Older strata

Lava flows

Lava fields -
old and not so old

The volcanoes which were active when the northern granites formed and the central complex erupted were not the only ones to affect the region. On at least five earlier occasions, volcanoes erupted and left their mark. The most widespread formed in the Carboniferous period, as part of a vast area of volcanoes which stretched to the Campsies north-east of Glasgow and beyond. Time and again large fissure volcanoes flooded the area with basalt lavas building up a pile many hundreds of metres thick. The south end of Bute and almost all of Little Cumbrae have 'trap featuring'. A few of the lavas reached Arran where they can be seen on the Corrie shore.

Other volcanic episodes left lavas and ashes on Arran; these are associated with both the Old and New Red Sandstone and Carboniferous rocks. The very oldest lavas are of the Ordovician age. These pillow lavas erupted under water, providing evidence that the area was covered by an ocean at that time.

Pillow lava, Corrie shore, Arran

Ancient folded rocks - the Scottish Highlands

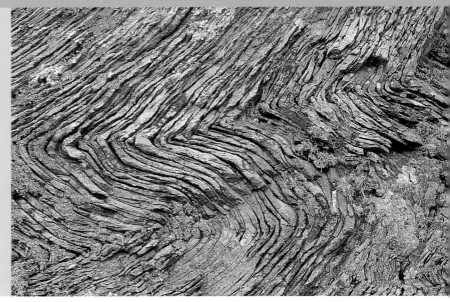

Folded schist, Imacher Point, Arran

North Arran and north Bute are actually part of the Scottish Highlands, made of rocks known as the Dalradian which occur in much of the region south-east of the Great Glen. The name originates from the ancient Scots kingdom of Dalriada. These rocks have characteristics which reveal a geological history quite different to that of Lowland Scotland. They are much older and, above all, they have been twisted and baked providing testimony to great upheavals in the Earth's crust.

The Dalradian rocks started life as conglomerates, sandstones, siltstones, mudstones, limestones and even lavas. They were laid down some 600 million years ago at the edge of an ocean called Iapetus, which lay in the Southern Hemisphere. To the north was a major continent known as Laurentia, forerunner to North America and Greenland as well as Scotland. Movement of the plates which form the Earth's crust gradually widened the ocean and moved the neighbouring continent of Gondwana (parts of which are seen today in England, Europe and North Africa) further away from Laurentia.

However, by 500 million years ago these movements reversed and the ocean became narrower. Chains of volcanic islands, similar to those in the present-day Pacific, were squashed against the edge of Laurentia as the continents moved towards each other. Collision of the continents produced the great Earth movements known as the Caledonian Orogeny. Buckling and thickening of the Earth's crust resulted in a mountain chain comparable to the present-day Alps or Himalayas. These mountains stretched for many thousands of kilometres and remnants are seen today in the Appalachians of North America, in East Greenland and in Scandinavia, as well as in the Scottish Highlands.

The rocks which were to become north Arran and Bute were buried at depths of 20 kilometres in the centre of the mountain chain. There they were heated to temperatures of up to 600°C; sandstones were altered to white quartzites, mudstones and shales to green schists and slates. The once flat-lying strata were folded, once, twice, several times over. This complex folding can be worked out on a grand, mountain-sized scale across north Arran. It can also be seen in miniature in the rocks exposed today. The pressure that produced the folding formed a new layering called cleavage; this is best seen in the way slates for roofing can be easily split along the closely spaced planes.

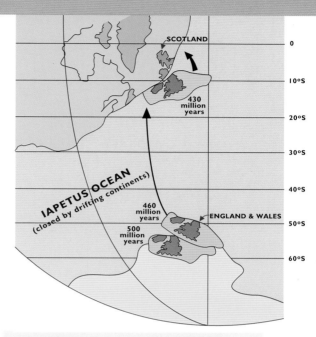

Iapetus Ocean - Scotland and England collide

The mountain chain has, over many millions of years, been worn down to its roots. The hard rocks so revealed produce bare craggy uplands with thin acid soils. The hills of Bute, north of the valley of Loch Fad, show this well. These Dalradian rocks also form a fringe of lower ground with rounded hills around the granite massif in north Arran.

In Bute, the valley between Kames Bay and Ettrick Bay lies where a band of softer rocks, mainly schists and slates, has been worn down more than the harder quartzites which form the hills to north and south.

Edge of the Highlands

A very old fracture in the Earth's crust marks the edge of the Highland rocks, where they have been brought against the younger, less altered rocks of the Midland Valley. Here, too, over 400 million years ago, an ancient ocean was squeezed and buried, and only thin slices of its rocks remain along the crack. This feature is known as the Highland Boundary Fault; it stretches from Stonehaven to Kintyre, crossing both Arran and Bute.

Highland Boundary Fault, Loch Fad, Bute

Highland Boundary Fault, Bute

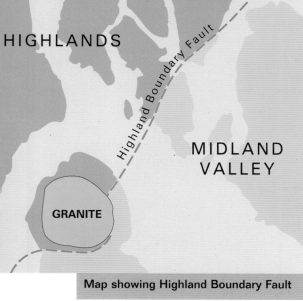

HIGHLANDS

Highland Boundary Fault

MIDLAND VALLEY

GRANITE

Map showing Highland Boundary Fault

Where the fault crosses Bute, erosion has picked out the softer fractured rocks and formed a valley. The ends are flooded to form Rothsay Bay and Scalpsie Bay, and in between is mostly filled by Loch Fad (long loch) and Loch Quien. Either side of this feature the landscape shows a marked contrast: to the north the typically bare craggy 'Highland' scenery; to the south the more gentle, fertile scenery of softer sedimentary and volcanic rocks.

In Arran the granite has exploited the weak zone of the Highland Boundary Fault plane and partly consumed it. As a result, the fault does not form a feature but can be followed by the junction of Highland and Midland Valley rocks both inland from Sannox and across the island just south of the granite.

Hutton's Section

Hutton's unconformity, Newton Point, Lochranza, Arran

When, in 1787, James Hutton, the Edinburgh scientist later to be hailed the founder of modern geology, came to Arran, the science of geology was in its infancy. Many problems had still to be solved, many new ideas formulated. So Arran's varied geology provided fertile ground for Hutton's active mind.

Still very much associated with him is the shore locality at North Newton which bears his name. Here, Hutton observed the angular discordance between two different types of strata now called an unconformity. He was able to deduce that it must have taken several geological processes over a very long period of time to give such a structure in the rocks. These were radical and even heretical opinions for his time.

The granite hills of north Arran and the way they pushed up through the sedimentary strata also provided a wealth of new information for Hutton. The splendid section through the north of the island, drawn by his artist friend, John Clerk of Eldin, was intended for his epic work, *Theory of the Earth.*

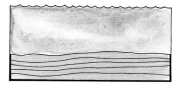

Chapter 1. The oldest rocks were laid down at the bottom of deep seas. The sediments were buried and became rocks.

Chapter 2. Continents moving closed the sea and squeezed the rocks till the strata were almost vertical, heated them so they became hard and pushed them up to form mountains.

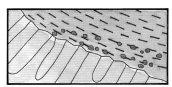

Chapter 3. The mountains were worn down by rain, flood, river, wind, trimming off the top of the strata. Torrents and freshwater floods carried boulders, gravel and sands and deposited them on top of the folded rocks.

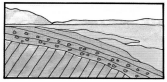

Chapter 4. Erosion wore down the mountains again to the position we see today.

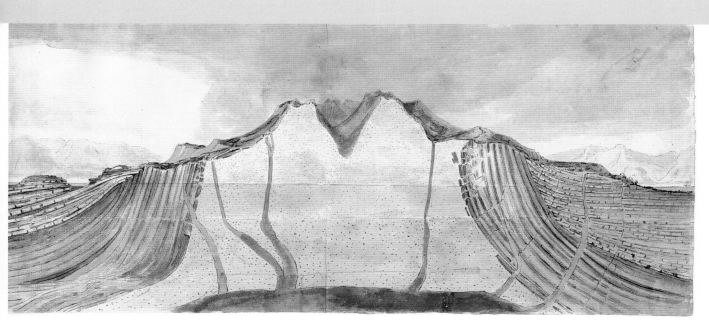

Detailed E-W section, Northern Granite, Isle of Arran (with acknowledgement to Sir John Clerk of Penicuik)

Sedimentary sandwich

Igneous rocks form the high ground; conversely the sedimentary rocks underlie the low ground. Quite simply, this is because layered strata like sandstones, siltstones and mudstones are not as hard as the igneous rocks and are worn down more quickly by erosion, be it by ice, water or wind. Thus the south part of Arran is mostly lower ground and there is a marked change in height between the granite hills and the sedimentary rocks which fringe them to the west and south.

The strata which form the south part of Arran and the middle of Bute are a sort of geological sandwich that tells us a lot about the different environment in which the rocks formed. Two red layers speak of harsh, arid deserts, and are known to geologists as the Old Red Sandstone and the New Red Sandstone, with a grey filling of Carboniferous strata telling of a more pleasant, tropical, forested environment. This can best be seen along the coast at the village of Corrie on Arran, with Old Red Sandstone to the north, the Carboniferous in the village and New Red Sandstone to the south - indeed all round the southern half of Arran.

Conglomorate, Craigmore shore, Bute

The Old Red Sandstone tells of a time when the Caledonian mountains lay to the north-west, and a vast desert plain to the south-east. Hit by sudden torrential showers, flash-floods ripped their way down from the mountains and deposited sands and gravels in the plains. Wind blew the sands into dunes. Temporary rivers flowed and lakes developed, only to dry up when the rain ceased. Thus the red sandstones, pebbly sandstones and conglomerates of the Old Red Sandstone were formed. These rocks form a belt across Arran round the south of the granite hills. On Bute they form the middle ground between the Highland hills in the north and the Carboniferous lava hills.

In the Carboniferous times as in the Midland Valley, sand from the rivers became sandstone, peat from the forests became coal, and lime from the coral reefs became limestone, which was later mined. On Arran and Bute, though, only a thin sequence is present as the islands lay on the edge of the area where these rocks were being deposited.

These rocks were squeezed to form hills. In Permian times torrential storms caused flash floods which wore down these hills and laid coarse breccias, gravels and sands in the plains. Wind picked up the sand and formed dunes which made their way across the Sahara-like desert; cross-beds from these dunes can be seen on the shore at Corrie. Under a magnifying glass individual grains can be seen to have been rounded by the wind.

Extensive plains developed, finer sands, silts and clays were deposited in lagoons and lakes which temporarily dried out leaving mudcracks, salt deposits and other features found in an arid landscape. Some life did colonise the area and left tracks preserved in the soft mud.

For at least some of the next 200 million years the region basked in the warmth of tropical seas, but the climate changed abruptly in the recent geological past with the onset of the Ice Age.

Corrie shore, Arran   **Sand dunes, Namibia**

Ice carves out valleys and corries

During the Ice Age a succession of ice sheets and mountain glaciers covered Scotland. The ice was not stationary, but moved leaving scratches called striae on the rocks, as stones and boulders in the base of the ice acted like a gigantic sheet of sand-paper. The ice flowed south from the Highlands over the region, scouring out deep hollows in the Kyles of Bute and on either side of Arran. The ice, too, picked out the softer rocks and left the harder volcanic rocks like granite, dolerite and felsite upstanding.

U-shaped valley, Glen Sannox, Arran

Throughout this period, valley glaciers carved out typical alpine valleys such as Glen Rosa. Alternate freezing and thawing of the rocks on the higher ground, combined with the glacial action, created the typical mountain hollows known as corries after the Gaelic word for these features. Where two corries erode towards each other, the result can be a saw-toothed ridge called an arête such as A' Chir, the cock's comb. These effects of glaciation are particularly noticeable in the granite hills.

Mounds of glacial debris called moraines were abandoned in the lower parts of the glaciated valleys, when the ice melted. The ground moraine (glacial till) left by the last ice-sheet covers much of the low ground of south and west Arran. Rocks and boulders were rounded and carried by the ice, sometimes long distances from their source; rock fragments from Ailsa Craig have been found as far afield as Pembrokeshire in South Wales. These are called erratics (wanderers) and large ones can form spectacular features.

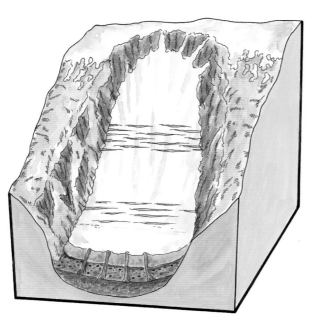

Glacier melts, depositing mounds of debris on the valley floor.

Kyles of Bute

When the sea was even higher

Raised beach Dougarie, Arran

All the Clyde islands have a more or less complete fringe of flat ground round them. Much of the road round Arran, for example, runs along this flat area, which lies only a few metres above sea level. It may be only a few metres wide or a broad plain, and is commonly backed by cliffs. This is a feature called a raised beach and dates back about 6,000 years to a time when the sea was higher than it is at present. This is because the world sea level rises and falls with the increase and decrease in the size of ice caps during ice ages and also because the land 'rebounds' slowly after the weight of ice is removed. These changes are still happening, so the islands are still rising out of the sea!

The Haystack, Scalpsie Bay, Bute

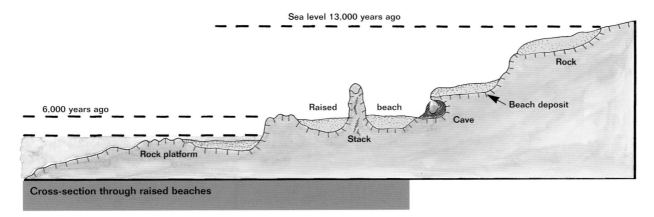

Sea level 13,000 years ago

Rock

6,000 years ago

Raised   beach

Beach deposit

Cave

Stack

Rock platform

Cross-section through raised beaches

This raised beach exactly mirrors the present beach, but at a higher level. Right at the end of the Ice Age the sea was up to about 30 metres higher than it is now, and there are deposits and features at several heights up to this level, particularly where there were broad estuaries like those behind Brodick, Loch Ranza and Lamlash. There are sand and shingle beach deposits, wave-cut platforms in rock, sea-stacks, and cliffs with sea-caves at different levels.

The Shiskine valley was once a broad estuary and Torr Righ was an island. Indeed, at the end of the Ice Age, Bute was three islands, at least at high tide when the sea flooded the valleys between Kames Bay and Ettrick Bay in the north and between Rothesay Bay and Scalpsie Bay including Loch Fad and Loch Quien in the south.

Sea-stacks vary in shape depending on the rock. Lion Rock and Diel's Dyke on Great Cumbrae are narrow ridges formed by large dolerite dykes. In contrast The Haystack on Bute is round because it is formed out of a uniform conglomerate.

King's Cave worn from Old Red Sandstone, west coast, Arran.

19

Man - mining and quarrying

Arran, Bute and the Cumbraes can claim to be largely unspoilt and their landscape unaffected by mining, quarrying or tipping. However, peat cutting, which still continues as a source of fuel, has changed the appearance since the last Ice Age.

Mining has occurred but has been restricted to a few small operations. The Corrie Limestone, which was excavated to form the Old Harbour, was quarried inland and mined from adits which can still be seen today (DO NOT ENTER - these are dangerous). An old limestone quarry at Kilchattan on Bute is now used as a reservoir.

Limestone mine opening, Corrie, Arran

Curling stone made of granite quarried from Ailsa Craig

Coal was mined in the Laggan and Cock of Arran area, and on Bute at Ascog and Loch Quien. Baryte, a heavy barium mineral, was mined in Glen Sannox during the last century and between the World Wars. Spoil heaps litter the valley floor, giving opportunities to hunt for minerals.

Many small quarries have been worked for building stones, such as the red and white sandstones. The igneous rocks, particularly the dolerite sills, have been worked for aggregate and road metal. Lastly, the Ailsa Craig microgranite has proved to be ideal for the manufacture of curling stones and has been quarried over many years for that purpose.

Recreation - climbing, cycling and geological excursions

Mountaineering

The northern hills present a fine challenge for mountaineers and ridge-walkers as well as the rambler. The well-jointed rock with its rough surface provides excellent climbing conditions. The bare rock and the sharp arête ridges result directly from the recent glaciation.

Study of Geology

Arran with its 'Scotland in miniature' variety of geology has, since the time of Hutton, been a magnet for geologists. Recently this has been particularly so for the undergraduate geologist, many of whom have had their first taste of real 'field' geology on Arran. Students are reminded of the need to conserve the many important localities described in this booklet, for the benefit of future generations by leaving their hammers on the bus (or better still, at home) and also of the need to ask permission to visit sites on private property

Remember to follow the Geological Code - see page 26.

Hillwalkers, Glen Rosa, Arran

Curling

This section would be incomplete without a mention of that traditional Scottish game, the 'roaring' game of curling and the part played by Ailsa Craig. The particular riebeckite microgranite long proved an ideal material for the perfect curling stone.

Cycling

The milestones are a feature of Arran, marking the 55.6 mile coast road, as well as the String and Ross roads. Nowadays easily travelled in a few hours, the traditional and still probably the best way to circumnavigate the island is by bicycle (or tricycle or tandem) and the milestones act as an encouragement and incentive. By cycle one can appreciate the geology and how the geology affects the nature, and the gradient, of the road.

Look out for the red sandstone milestones, reputedly from the Old Red Sandstone quarries at Corrie.

Arran milestone

Arran Map

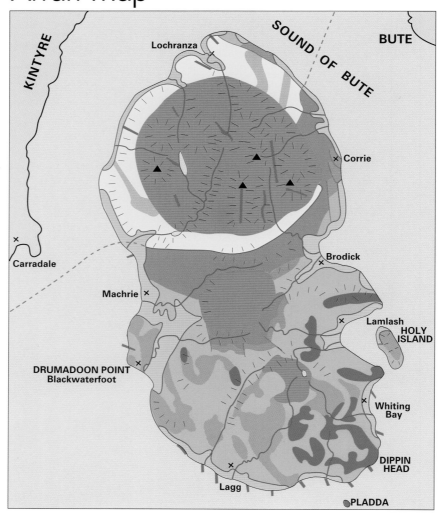

KINTYRE

SOUND OF BUTE

BUTE

Lochranza

Corrie

Carradale

Brodick

Machrie

Lamlash

HOLY
ISLAND

DRUMADOON POINT
Blackwaterfoot

Whiting
Bay

DIPPIN
HEAD

Lagg

PLADDA

Raised beach feature
and deposits

New Red Sandstone

Carboniferous
sedimentary rocks

Carboniferous volcanic rocks

Old Red Sandstone

Bute and Cumbraes Map

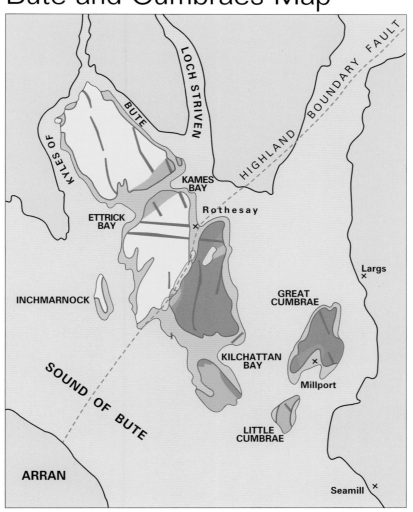

LOCH STRIVEN

HIGHLAND BOUNDARY FAULT

KYLES OF BUTE

KAMES BAY

Rothesay

ETTRICK BAY

Largs

GREAT CUMBRAE

INCHMARNOCK

KILCHATTAN BAY

Millport

SOUND OF BUTE

LITTLE CUMBRAE

ARRAN

Seamill

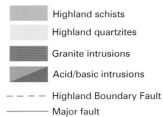 Highland schists

Highland quartzites

Granite intrusions

Acid/basic intrusions

– – – – Highland Boundary Fault

——— Major fault

Geological time-scale

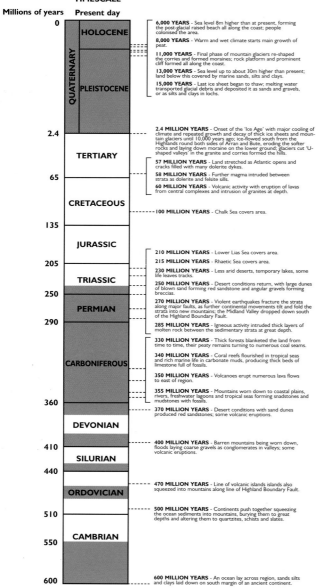

TIMESCALE

Millions of years — **Present day**

0	

QUATERNARY

HOLOCENE

6,000 YEARS - Sea level 8m higher than at present, forming the post-glacial raised beach all along the coast; people colonised the area.

8,000 YEARS - Warm and wet climate starts main growth of peat.

11,000 YEARS - Final phase of mountain glaciers re-shaped the corries and formed moraines; rock platform and prominent cliff formed all along the coast.

13,000 YEARS - Sea level up to about 30m higher than present; land below this covered by marine sands, silts and clays.

15,000 YEARS - Last ice sheet began to thaw; melting water transported glacial debris and deposited it as sands and gravels, or as silts and clays in lochs.

PLEISTOCENE

2.4

2.4 MILLION YEARS - Onset of the 'Ice Age' with major cooling of climate and repeated growth and decay of thick ice sheets and mountain glaciers until 10,000 years ago; ice-flowed south from the Highlands round both sides of Arran and Bute, eroding the softer rocks and laying down moraine on the lower ground; glaciers cut 'U-shaped valleys' in the granite and corries formed the hills.

TERTIARY

57 MILLION YEARS - Land stretched as Atlantic opens and cracks filled with many dolerite dykes.

65

58 MILLION YEARS - Further magma intruded between strata as dolerite and felsite sills.

60 MILLION YEARS - Volcanic activity with eruption of lavas from central complexes and intrusion of granites at depth.

CRETACEOUS

100 MILLION YEARS - Chalk Sea covers area.

135

JURASSIC

210 MILLION YEARS - Lower Lias Sea covers area.

205

215 MILLION YEARS - Rhaetic Sea covers area.

230 MILLION YEARS - Less arid deserts, temporary lakes, some life leaves tracks.

TRIASSIC

250 MILLION YEARS - Desert conditions return, with large dunes of blown sand forming red sandstone and angular gravels forming breccias.

250

270 MILLION YEARS - Violent earthquakes fracture the strata along major faults, as further continental movements tilt and fold the strata into new mountains; the Midland Valley dropped down south of the Highland Boundary Fault.

PERMIAN

285 MILLION YEARS - Igneous activity intruded thick layers of molten rock between the sedimentary strata at great depth.

290

330 MILLION YEARS - Thick forests blanketed the land from time to time, their peaty remains turning to numerous coal seams.

340 MILLION YEARS - Coral reefs flourished in tropical seas and rich marine life in carbonate muds, producing thick beds of limestone full of fossils.

CARBONIFEROUS

350 MILLION YEARS - Volcanoes erupt numerous lava flows to east of region.

355 MILLION YEARS - Mountains worn down to coastal plains, rivers, freshwater lagoons and tropical seas forming snadstones and mudstones with fossils.

360

370 MILLION YEARS - Desert conditions with sand dunes produced red sandstones; some volcanic eruptions.

DEVONIAN

400 MILLION YEARS - Barren mountains being worn down, floods laying coarse gravels as conglomerates in valleys; some volcanic eruptions.

410

SILURIAN

440

470 MILLION YEARS - Line of volcanic islands islands also squeezed into mountains along line of Highland Boundary Fault.

ORDOVICIAN

500 MILLION YEARS - Continents push together squeezing the ocean sediments into mountains, burying them to great depths and altering them to quartzites, schists and slates.

510

CAMBRIAN

550

600

600 MILLION YEARS - An ocean lay across region, sands silts and clays laid down on south margin of an ancient continent.